# TEB Like 123

Stephen J. Terrell

Shiri Sher

Dedicated to our children:

Luke and John Michael

Elichai, Shalomi, Kiki, Aliya, and Azarya

# An Introduction: What is TEB?

Welcome to Transforming the Experience-Based Brain (TEB), a modality of bringing greater awareness to our nervous system that may have been disrupted early in life.  The field of psychology has grown leaps and bounds in grasping the important connection between trauma and its direct impact on the body.  We now understand that trauma is not just experienced emotionally but has a physiological component that needs repair.  The somatic therapeutic approaches have all grown as a result of this need.  TEB, in particular, mirrors the attachment between parent and child, which is literally the mainframe upon which all attachments, relationships, and a sense of security within a child, is built.  As repairs to attachment occur, the individual's nervous system begins to settle, and increases its capacity for resilience.

Through my work with children in foster care as well as those who are being prepared for adoption or post-adoption, our nervous system becomes our primary focus in the effort of healing.  Our nervous system's earliest memory is often that of fear which then becomes a lifelong struggle towards safety. A myriad of fight and flight responses ensue as the body struggles in a state of dysregulation. This can look like acting out, anxiety, depression, turning to addictive substances, and even acts of crime, all desperate acts of the body which thirsts for a sense of equilibrium.  TEB very gently and carefully guides the body back towards its true state of equilibrium, a regulated nervous system that is no longer in fight or flight mode.

Come along with us as we move towards repair and find our way, creating new neural pathways that allow us to gently change our way of being.

As you hold your child's hand today, or hold them in your arms, may these words open the door to something special and beautiful between you and your child.

Stephen J. Terrell PsyD, founder of TEB
Co-Author of *Nurturing Resilience: Helping Clients Move Forward from Developmental Trauma*
To find out more information on TEB visit austinattach.com

There's a connection
that we can't see.
An invisible line
between you and me.

Our body, it knows,
and it feels this bond,
that makes us feel grounded
and helps us feel strong.

Regulation,
in the body machine,
the natural hum
that's felt but not seen.

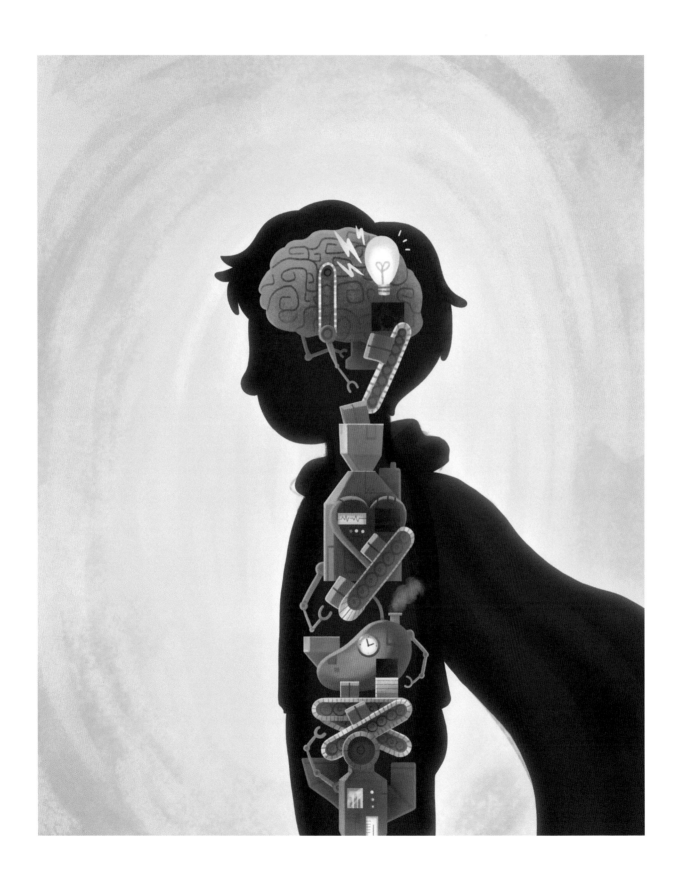

When you just feel right
and you're feeling great,
Your body hums,
It radiates!

And 123, that's TEB!

What happens then,
when you're feeling off?
And even if you try
with all your might,
your body's just not
feeling right?

That's dysregulation!

That natural hum
has gone away.
And your body just does
not feel ok.

Let's take a moment...
And 123...
We give it a boost with TEB!

Are you ready to take this journey with me?

Feel free to lie back,
let your body arrive.
Transforming your
experience,
let's take a dive!

We start with
the heart center,
and we give it more space.
Allowing more opening,
allowing more grace.

We move to the kidneys and adrenals, their hats, spreading love and intention.

What a yummy connection!

We cradle the head,
where the brain stem hides.
Filling it with
the love and light
that's spreading inside.

And now to the ankles,
They are hinges, you see.
The "ickiness" is released
and we feel more free!

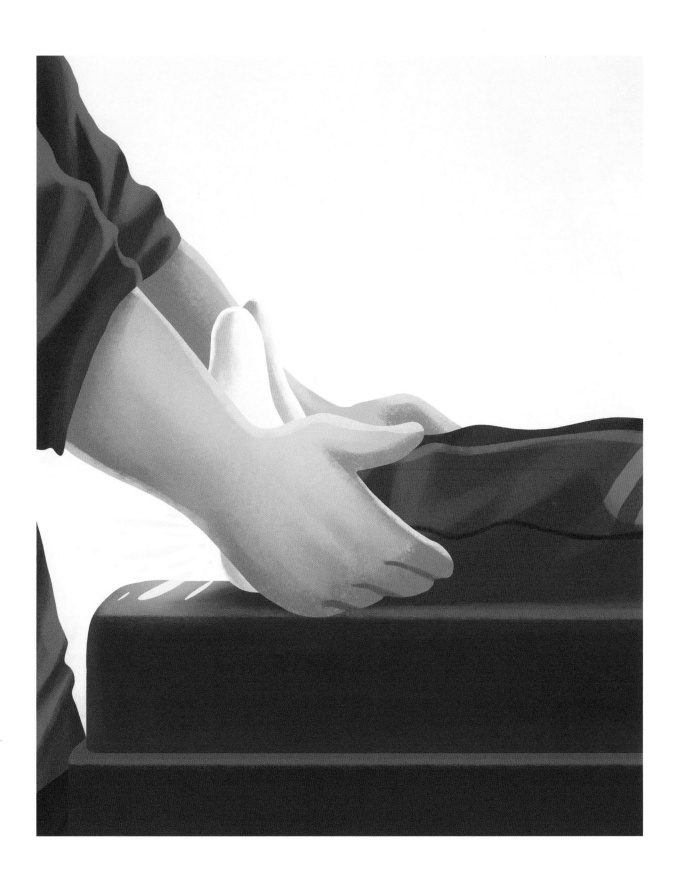

Closing with
the Limbic Installation.

What a sensation!

Toes in and rest.
Pushing out and rest.

And before I know it,
I'm starting to feel like
my best!

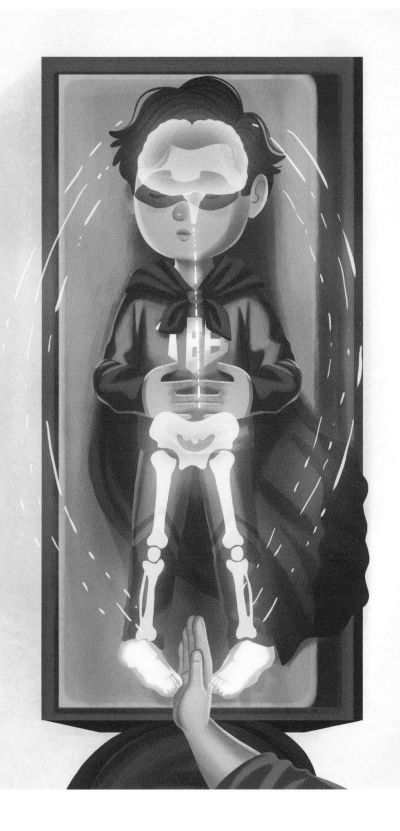

Two minutes of silence.

My body's gears are turning.
My insides are churning.
In this quiet still place,
in this sacred space,
my body is healing.
It's an amazing feeling.

TEB like 123
I feel better in my body!

Thankful to the Creator,
Whose Infinite Wisdom
and Grace,
made my body
with the ability
to heal itself.

We give it support,
and nurture the bond.
We give the body space,
and with God's help,
healing takes place.

That's TEB, like 123,
Supporting that
invisible bond
Between you and me.

# About the Authors:

**STEPHEN J. TERRELL, PsyD, SEP**, is a leading expert in the field of Developmental Trauma and Adoption. The founder of the Austin Attachment and Counseling Center, Terrell works directly with individuals and families affected by trauma and teaches throughout the United States, Japan, and Europe. A Licensed Professional Counselor (Texas) with a background in Somatic Experiencing® and EMDR, he has also been a featured keynote speaker at international adoption conferences and presenter at attachment and play therapy conferences. Terrell lives in Pflugerville, Texas. To find out more about Steve check out his website austinattach.com

**SHIRI SHER** is the author of several children's books on spirituality and mindfulness. As she was raising her children, she wanted to impart important values and life lessons, so she used storytelling to teach and simplify these often-complex ideas. This is her first therapeutic children's book. Shiri has a BA in psychology and did graduate level work in art therapy. She worked extensively with the at-risk youth and developed programs for their unique needs. She currently works with individuals using a variety of therapeutic modalities, such as voice dialogue facilitation and Transforming Touch, as a TEB practitioner. She lives in New Jersey with her husband and five children. To get in touch, reach out on her website shirisher.com

Printed in Great Britain
by Amazon

25119723R00023